About the Author

Zoey Allard lives in London, and is working towards a university degree in Psychology and Criminology. Her early years were dedicated to studying English Literature and she was always fascinated by writing. She was invested in the craft of poetry, she found it to be therapeutic. She discovered that it spoke volumes for those who lost their own voice at some time and it helped her get past a difficult time in her life. Writing poetry allowed her to be creative and artistic as she started writing about unspoken truths of society.

All the Words I Wish You Said

Zoey Allard

All the Words I Wish You Said

Vanguard Press

VANGUARD PAPERBACK

© Copyright 2024
Zoey Allard

The right of Zoey Allard to be identified as author of this work has been asserted by her in accordance with the Copyright, Designs and Patents Act 1988.

All Rights Reserved

No reproduction, copy or transmission of this publication may be made without written permission.
No paragraph of this publication may be reproduced, copied or transmitted save with the written permission of the publisher, or in accordance with the provisions of the Copyright Act 1956 (as amended).

Any person who commits any unauthorised act in relation to this publication may be liable to criminal prosecution and civil claims for damages.

A CIP catalogue record for this title is available from the British Library.

ISBN 978 1 83794 175 9

Vanguard Press is an imprint of
Pegasus Elliot Mackenzie Publishers Ltd.
www.pegasuspublishers.com

First Published in 2024

Vanguard Press
Sheraton House Castle Park
Cambridge England

Printed & Bound in Great Britain

To those that have made me the person I am today, to the noble teachers that I admire. Thank you for noticing the dorky kid at the back of the class and helping me reach my potential. To Mr Colenzo, Ms Gregory, Mr Holman, Ms Vowels, Mr Spragg. To my sister, Amal, my role model and inspiration. Thank you for essentially raising me, this book would not have happened without you. Thank you to my family for supporting my dream.

This collection of verse is very special and personal to me as an individual and as a poet. It is my collection of experiences as a young woman living in a turbulent society, and in turbulent times. Thank you to the publishers and editors for making this dream a reality. A big thank you to Pegasus for giving new writers the opportunity and for recognising my work and talent. As Dickens once said, "Suffering has been stronger than all other teaching, and has taught me to understand what your heart used to be. I have been bent and broken, but – I hope – into a better shape." — Great Expectations

All the Words I Wish You Said

As cliché as it sounds
Tell me you love me
That you need me
That you want me.

Say those pretty three words
Like a chant, a mantra
"I love you"
I'll never hear those words enough.

As cliché as it is
Those are the words; I wish, you said
Early morning, late in bed
All those mundane moments filled with love are missed.

Like words; I wish you said
Like a chant; a mantra
Over and over again
Just to hear you, to know you are there.

"I will be by your side: always and forever"
Those are the words; I wish you said.

From Mr to Mrs

Read my lips
They call for you
I want your heart to do flips
Like mine does
When you look into my eyes
You remind me; why I fell in love
With everything about you
From your long Auburn tresses to
Your chocolate syrup eyes
Dripping with love
How long do I have to wait before you love me too?
This time it's real
This time I give myself to you.

Gift

Her:
On my doorstep is a small bundle;
Of colour vivid and bright
The pinks, reds and yellows blending
Into the colour of that sunset.

Him:
The colour of that sunset
Embedded, laced and stitched onto every memory of ours
The rose tinted cheeks, your sun-kissed skin and pearly lipped
All in that bundle by the door.

Her:
Holding them close to my chest
Almost feeling your warmth
As cliché as it is, I feel you beside me
I remember being warmed at your words.

Him:
That day, cold as ice
But your pleading face could take me anywhere
By the beach in your sweater
We could see the sunset.

Her:
That day, cold as ice
Warmth spread far and wide
When you asked me to be your wife.

The Kiss

Nothing could stop us,
There was no discussion
No rationality could stop the passion erupting
It would only be corrupting.

Your hands tracing the curves and planes on me
Melting into the moment of passion
Letting you embrace me with those strong arms
Letting you hold me.

I will never feel those hands again
I will never forget the feeling of your hands
We were free
Though you might not agree.

Go on, kiss me again
Go on, hold me again
Go on, look me in the eyes again
Go on, just say that you miss me again
Just once more time.

Just one last time.

Through Health and Sickness; Through Hell or Heaven for All of Eternity I Am Yours

The ache in my heart
The burn across my skin
Scalding are your finger tips
As the bindings tighten.

"Promise you'll never leave."
The question rings in my mind
The binding tightens
Burning my skin.

Plucking my wings
Snatching my voice
I took solace in another man's arms
The bindings have a golden hue.

No longer with a halo
But with horns
I do your bidding
As the bindings tighten.

The marks of bondage never leave
Even though I am long gone
The redness on my ring finger is etched on
"I promise to never leave."

Through Health and Sickness; Through Hell or Heaven for All Eternity You Are Mine

The dried tears on your face
The etched mark of the mace
Scalding are my finger tips
As I tighten the bindings.

"Promise you'll never leave."
I make sure the question rings in your head
I tighten the bindings
Scarring your precious skin.

Plucking your wings
Ripping your voice
Seeing you run away
You'll never find solace in anyone else.

No longer an angel
You have fallen from grace
You will do my bidding
As the bindings tighten.

May the scars be etched on forever
Even though you are gone
Scarred is your skin.
You cannot leave
Not now. Not ever.

Azure

Looking into your azure eyes
All I see is my smiling reflection
Looking into your azure eyes,
All I feel is your affection.

The sizzle in the air
The hum of our breaths
Unaware
Of how it would change, unaware of the stress.

When I see you, all I want to see is your blush
The rosy tint matching your lips. Yearning for you again and again
It comes back with a rush
I need to abstain.

Abstain. Abstain.
From you, your peevish smile, the twinkle in your eyes,
Can't lose the butterflies
When I look into your azure eye.

Name

There every second of the day
There in my space-
What is my space?
"I need you out."

Voice meek and quivering
It's all that comes out
Battered and bruised
Lips busted and bleeding
The air filled with the pungent scent
Voice shattered
Crushed with your bare hands
Looking down at me
Curled on the concrete.

"I need you out."
But we are already out
My skin bitten and nipped by the cold air
The concrete scratching my bruised flesh
Wounds already scabbing over
Is it over?

Not yet-
As his fingers slithering onto my scalp
Latching on to my hair like leeches
After blood

Like parasites
Eroding their hosts
Until they don't know their name anymore.

All I hear is his gutteral laugh as I stutter away;
"What's your name?"

Fix You

My new project,
Something not quite broken
Something not quite healed
New and old all at once.

My new project,
Is your broken heart
That I'll fix
Hoping you'll love me.

Fixing yours, instead of mine
You have all my attention
All my love
I don't need any for myself.

This new project,
Like every cycle, like every loop
Ends and starts again
With you I'll be done soon
Forget and then run away.

Almost that I can't accept your love
Even though that's all I wanted
I'll blame it on the love I never got
But let me fix you, just like how I was taught.

Notice

I tell you pretty lies
I tell you that I don't care
Under the skies of guises
Because I know you would sneer.

I tell you pretty lies
So that you will care
Living under a disguise
Just so you would stare.

I tell you pretty lies
Do I seem pretty?
In your eyes
Pretty as those girls in the city.

I tell you pretty lies
Do you notice?
You despise my pretty lies
You can tell it's bogus.

I can't stop telling you pretty lies
Because you'll forget me
There is no compromise
I know you'll never notice me

But I have always noticed you.

Neon Smiles

Neon signs
At midnight
The jukebox humming in the corner
Sitting Infront of my American breakfast
Wondering how the time passed me by.

The neon signs faltering
Just as my smile did
Promising to call again
Promising to never lose you.

The weight in my chest leaves when you are around
So please don't go
Don't leave me alone
The weight will never leave.

I wanna drown:
Drown in booze
Drown in your eyes
Instead I drown the pancakes
Soak to the core
Just like the one rainy night.

Maybe I should jump on the next flight
Maybe you didn't want to fight
Maybe I should give up hope, give up the light
Maybe I should jump from this height.

Deal

If I could make a deal with God
To take your hurt and pain away
Even though He is just a fraud
It's better than seeing you drink every day.

Blighted is your heart so
That you forgot the words you once said to me
Blighting my heart so
When you beg me to set you free.

The irony of the commandments
The irony of condemnation
The irony of Hell
The irony of Heaven.

Smelling like spirits
You pray for it to be over
For God's hand to strike retribution
I pray for it to be over.

Just say those words to me once more; before you leave:
'You're my angel'

Past My Time

I want to stay
I sound like a child whose begging to play
The same pleading, whining
The same unyielding pining.

My darling
My love
I want to stay
But that frown on your face says everything.

I promised you:
When the world is ending, I'll be by your side
In your pain: I'll be by your side
Yet I left you so early.

Your disapproving stare says everything
You want me to suffer no longer
You'd rather suffer than I
I know you, but I still want to stay past my time.

No bright shining light can take me
No shinigami
No Osiris
No Thanatos
No horned god of death
Can take me away from my love.

I will stay past my time
I will guard, what once was mine.

It

It happened
Should I be happy or sad?
Should I weep or laugh?
It's bubbling up inside me.

You know it-
That feeling that claws at your heart
Sinking each nail in before dragging it down
The blood oozing and pouring
Pouring into an emptied chalice.

Every step is dizzying
The lights blurring and fuzzy
Nothing sits quite straight
I watch time with a bated breath.

Taking each step with a prep
A bounce, A giggle
It's brought that out of me.

It's brought out the best in me
The part that smiles and coos
The part is in complete servitude
I am hers, that little bundle of joy

Disorientating and dizzying.

Her smile gnaws at my heart
Heart-wrenching
Dressed in Lilies
Pale as snow.

Cheeks tinted with rose
To know you from it to her-
For you to become my truth
Blinding reason
Seeing only fiery passion
My sweet; may you feel the same ache at the glimpse of
    your own bundle of joy.

Music to My Ears

Loving you was like a melody
So beautiful but just as fleeting
Loving you was like a song
That could never be sung
Loving you was like a loop
Endless, ringing in my mind
Loving you was like a harmony
That I was never allowed to have.

Cruel Prince

Oh my cruel prince
Hold me so in your humble embrace
And push me from a cliff
Your love is a bittersweet twist.

Your cruelty is your charm
You can only do me harm
The royal blood pumping in your veins
Taints my remains.

Cruel prince abdicate thy throne
It was all but known
The poison filling my chalice
Your cruelty, your malice.

Oh cruel prince
Thy blood-red crown is rinsed
Ready for its place a top of your head
Ready for more bloodshed.

Oh, my cruel prince,
I will fill your chalice with my own blood
Take me as your own
And let it be known
We have shared a humble embrace.

Pineapple

The forest green crown
Gracing the top of its head
Wearing a frown
As time sped.

The prickly cold words
The refreshing brutality
In the spring air; flying hummingbirds
Kind words are an abnormality.

Sickly sweet,
Yellow hue; just as the sun
The ripeness of: heart, mind and conceit
So he does know how to have fun.

My haughty cold lover
Though your smile rare, your kindness more admirable
Though your words brutal; your kindness more admirable
My haughty cold lover; struck and bruised you may be
But your core remains sweet, tangy and untainted
Like the sweetness of a bruised pineapple.

Tomorrow

Tomorrow
A day like any other
The same toothpaste, shampoo, conditioner
The same heartache.

Tomorrow
A day like any other
A day of a hollow smile, hollow heart
Tomorrow will be no better.

A day like any other,
Is a day of: senseless chatter, words with no meaning
    and empty promises
To be such a disappointment to my mother
Who raised me to live like there was no tomorrow.

I will carry on as I am,
With the same toothpaste, shampoo and conditioner
Ruining myself as I carry on
For as long as there is a tomorrow
There will be my hollow heart.

Hate

I wish the worst
I truly do
I wish for your heart to break, to shatter
I truly do.

I truly want to see your pain; your misery
It is beautiful
Adoring your pathetic little face
The sad puppy eyes, the feeble smile as you hold your tears back.

It's too funny, seeing you choke your tears down
It brings me overwhelming joy
As your lips tremble
As more and more callous words escape:
"Your welcome."

Staring

I've spent the day
Hidden away
Like a parasite
Sucking the joy and life.

Staring and commenting
Just because I can
My eyes bleeding from the harsh blue light
But I can't look away
Spine crumpled like paper
But I can't stop.

They told me it's okay
They told me it's cool
They said, it would be fine
So why do I hate myself?

The more I stare, the more I hate
It like a cycle, it was fate
It was written in the stars
That's what I tell myself to justify the scars.

The scabs decorating my nails
And the missing flesh on my arms
As I pinch
And bite.

And chew
On my skin
Eating my shell
As it eats my insides.

Hate gurgling in my stomach
Like acid
I feel nothing as I check the number of likes
Why don't they like me?
"Why are there only fifty-four likes; it's been four hours"
They said liked me!

The blood pours out with the sound of my heart beat
I'm nothing
I am hollow
I'm something swallowed;
Consumed - By the consumer.

Snob

Are you sick of my flowery language?
Does it sicken you?
Am I disgusting?
Repugnant? Filthy? Gross?

I can't help it
I've been taught to hide my truth in flowery lies
I can't help, that I've been taught to lie
I can't control it.

It's not my fault that my inner child wasn't suffocated
    with compliments
About more than just my complexion
Inner child still hungry to prove its worth
That intense begging
"Look at me", "Aren't I so smart?"
All of this left unfulfilled.

So now I brag and boast
Get validation from teachers
They call me "pet"; "show off";
The "snob"
It sickens them, why wouldn't it sicken you?

In my most honest words;
I'm just begging for love and attention

The one I was promised
The one I was robbed off.

The Doll

I keep it still
Hidden away in some corner
Throwing a hateful gaze in its direction.

I keep it still
Despite the memory
Etched into my mind
And the fear
I fight every day.

I keep it still
Arguing it's wasteful to throw it away
Maybe I'm too scared
Maybe I shouldn't be mad at it at all.

I keep it still
Maybe because it reminds me
To be wary
In case there are more of you
To fend off every day.

Dream

It's her again
Her figure looming over my bed
Looming over my life
It's just a dream.

Eyes blood-shot and translucent
Just like her figure
There but not quite
Her smile hollow and unnerving.

She bleeds slowly
Crimson red tears from her slit wrist
Following me with a trail of blood in her wake
Her body twisting, contorting into the unnatural

It's her; the intruder
Invading in the dreams of happy days
Her saliva thickened with my metallic blood
She smiles at me, when I awaken.

Hell Hath No Fury like a Woman Scorned

Years and years passed on
With a snap of my fingers
Roaming this earth
Lost and unfound.

I've become the plague
Black and putrid
Venomous pus oozing from my remains
Dried blood painting my veins.

I had my fun
Watching you suffer
The ache and pain
Of growing older
The chance you robbed me of.

Now centuries passed
I walk this house alone
In its glorious destruction
I seek solace ins silence.

One last deed looming in my mind
In this house; I will conjure
Fire blazing like my eternal wrath
May your eternal rest be restless.

Damned if...

Damned if I
Wear short skirts
Damned if I don't

Danmed if
Wear makeup
Damn if I
Damned if I like you
Damned if I don't.

It's almost like
My voice isn't even there
It's almost like
No one cares.

Pushing myself further and further
Until I forget
How sunlight caressed my skin
How trees danced, and flowers sung.

Pushing my head further and further down
Til air becomes a luxury
Damned if I fight and yell

Damned if I don't

Damned if I tell
Damned if I don't
I'll keep the secret
That weighs like a corpse.

Damn you
For stealing my voice
Damn you
For the weight on my shoulders
Damn you.

Choice

"You led them on."
"You were flirting with them."
"Whore" "slut"
"She deserved what she got."

My fault that I want to look pretty
Feel confident in my skin
As I go dance with my friends in the city
Next thing I know, I'm strapped to a hospital bed.

Test after test
Just to make sure; I wasn't lying
"Girls just want attention these days."
Excuses after excuses to poke and prod.

I want to raise my voice; to shriek
To scream and tell them
It was me not my clothes:
 that they raped
That they violated and tore.

Now-
I have no choice
But one
To return to God as an angel
Flying too close to the sun

And falling into the highway
Me and my baby as one.

The Mannequin

They change my clothes every day
The trends change
The ideal shape changes
One day, I'm the "it" girl
Next day, they want a replacement.

Staring out from the display
Where I'm caged
I see the girls
Staring, oggling, frowing
Shaming my figure.

Shame the cooperate world
Who sells me
Shame those who made me
Into the plastic I am
Shame me for being a fool.

Pleaser

Crowd pleaser
People pleaser
Feeling thrown into the freezer
Always teasing her.

Why not me?
Really making me put DUFF into use
Really making me wanna flee
Why can't I be your muse?

It's not funny, how you ignore me
It's not funny that you ask about my friends
It's not funny that I want to cry
It's not funny how I still want you

Crowd pleaser
People pleaser
Walk away just this once
Whatever dignity you have left

Crowd pleaser just hide yourself away.

Villain

She's cold and callous
She won't even look at you
She hates everyone and everything
She's such a buzz kill.

She makes the room temperature drop
She's hollow, empty inside
She makes want to give up and die
She's so silent you could hear a pin drop.

She stays away from big crowds
The one's that bark less bite more

It's okay, I'll be alone
I'll bear the burden in silence
Comfort in pain
I watch you scramble in fear.

Thinking I am twisted
I see the fear in your eyes
It used to bring me joy
But god- I don't know happened today.

I want to feel the sun
The warmth
I though the cold was liberating and cutting

But now it's just that- cold

Still you run away
As if I had set hellhounds to your chase
The ones that bite; and leave a trace.

Mirror

Everyone looks at it
Glances here and there
Some straighten their ties
Some fix their hair.

If everyone looks at it why can't I?
The dusty surface
Not even light can touch it
Hidden away in the corner of my room.

In the darkness of my room
Relief touches me
Free from reflections
Of my ugly visage.

Free from the blinding clarity
In which I see myself
Preferring the darkness to the light.

The baggy clothes
Act as my solace
No one can see the scars
Hidden under

Faltering as I walk past
Regretting the moment

I make contact with my own orbs
I see the mirror crack and shatter.

Sob Story

I'll tell you a sob story
It begins when my world began
A world where I didn't belong
A world where I was miserable
The story goes:
Let's bring a child into this world; let's show her the
 pain of being alive
Let's get her to strive
And crush all her hopes and dreams
Spoil her skin with luxurious creams
And blame her for wasting money
Let's bring a child into this world
So she can tell our sob story.

World Comes Crashing Down

To be that age
So fruitful and young
When it feels like the world is collapsing
When you have had your first kiss.

To be young is no longer the same
Instead of the feeling
The world Comes Crashing down
The weight crushes us.

I'm at this age
Where my every move is watched
Hated or loved
I'm at that age.

I'm at this age
Where the weight of the world is dawning on me
The age where nothing feels right
This age where everything is an argument, a fight.

This age
Didn't prepare for this weight
Unequipped for the barbaric massacre
That takes a friend
One at a time.

To rebel
To fight
This regime
I have neither swords nor guns
Just whatever is left of my voice.

Don't Breathe

Don't breathe
It's everywhere
The ocean, the soil, the air, in and out of you
Don't breathe.

Trickles of poison in our blood,
When we fight and scream, they call it a fuss
For their own luxury, that is superfluous
They sacrifice you and me; us.

They laugh and jeer
Calling it hocus pocus
They won't be laughing, when we all disappear.

Let it be known, let me say this here and now
Their poison trickling down into our chalice
Plaiting the coarse truth with glistening lies
Like gold plated corpses behind the factories.

Don't breathe-
Don't let them win
When we pass; amass
Time won't let them have the last laugh.

Nothing

That emptiness when you finish a book, movie, show
When you become the character
Living so vicariously
Through their eyes
I am nothing but that character
I am her, she is me
Her voice becomes my own
Her name; mine
Until she is haggard and worn
From her, I'll move on.

Ash

'Burnout'
Like ash to the ground
The red flames that consumed me
Eating my flesh;
Both alive
Only one prevailed.

Pricking my skin like a thousand needles
The endless heat and pressure charring my skin
I pushed through
It's all a 'test'
I will come out as a diamond
The one who withstood the pressure.

They lied, over and over again
Promising; 'Those burns are a sign of victory, a sign of endurance'
And I believed
Mindlessly.

Til the flames consumed and consumed
Until they had their fill of the mindless fool
And all there was left of me was –
Ashes.

To Protect

Whether you blame evolution or instinct
Our very nature dictates the protection of our young
Ingrained into us
Into our very biology.

Yet so many have failed
The parents of our parents
Leaving a legacy: of pain and heart break
Leaving a legacy: of failure.

And those
Who live up to their biology: who protect
Leave a sour taste: In our hearts

Envy and jealousy
Tainting the beauty of our essence
Cursing and hating
"They don't know what the real world is like."
Protected from the horrors of reality
And the monster under the bed
Nothing to fear;
Should be the life of a child.

That One Person

You know that one person?
The person you thought of immediately after reading that?
Yes, that person,
That person that brings light into your life?

Yes, I have known her since I was a child
That one person, who would give up anything to be with me
Who protected and sheltered me
Even though she herself was but a child

Raising me more as a mother than a sister
She is that one person,
Who is the reason I am alive.
My sister.

My sister,
Who I go to whether it be a good day or bad
Who loves me endlessly and blindly
Who tells me off for being stubborn.

She is that one person,
Who I love more than life itself
When I say I love her to the moon and back,
I mean I love her with every beat of my heart

She is my person.

The Sister

Sister, sister
With the rosy lips, tanned cheeks and honey dew eyes
Let me whisper
Our next disguise.

For when we prank our mother
Always partners in crime
Even when we tease our brother
It is perfect time.

For me to take ugly pictures
Of your sleeping face, of your ugly toes
It's an addiction
How many I have? Who knows.

And you, strumming my eyebrows whenever
Tickling me
Please let us like this forever
Whatever bribe you need, how much ever tea

Sister, sister
Stay with me
Sister sister
We've learned to be free
Sister, sister
You and me
Will always be

Partners in crime.

Brother, Brother

You are so annoying
Breathing down my neck
Curious as ever
As annoying as it, it's endearing.

I do wonder, often, what life would be like without
You annoy the living lights out of me.
It just seems like a bleak life
One without you would be incomplete-

Even though we don't say this as much as we should
Know I mean it when I say,
"You are so annoying."
but I never truly mean:
"Leave me alone!"

Now, Then, When

Now,
The world is ugly
Fighting, killing amongst their own
Now,
The world has no hope.

Then,
The time we idealise
But the world was still ugly
Ice cold, frozen solid, in its crystal reflection the truth is
    reflected
No, the world was still ugly.

When,
When the war is over
The blood dripping, bones crushed, chunks splattered across the walls
When the war is over,
We'll fear the next.

Where Are You From?

"Where are you from?"
Same question; new day; new person
My accent not from here
But somewhere foreign; exotic
"I can't quite put my finger on it."

I'm worldly
I come from the treasures of India
The olive tanned skin from the Arabs
The slants of my eyes inherently East Asian
I am ambiguity.

I am worldly
But from nowhere
I belong to no race, no denomination, no nation
I am merely a person.

To answer your question in short:
My accent is just that
My accent
Unique to me, to my voice
Like fingerprint
That can't be replicated.

Relic of My Blood

In my chalice,
Beyond worldly possessions
I hold you in me
Like a vessel of love.

What remains of you
Is a relic of my memory
Aged and worn
Through the decades.

They stole you,
Abducted, withheld,
Both you and I; Lovelorn
I languish still
For you who had been snatched.

Smell

Better than any essential oils,
The aroma of Lavender, tulips
Could never compare being in my mother's arms
The sweet smell of her sweat putting me to sleep.

The stench of her sweat, pungent and tangy
To any other
But to me,
It is sweet.

It makes me recall all those sleepless nights,
Of sickness and health
Of our time together
Where she sacrificed herself for me.

When she could be sleeping
Preparing for tomorrow,
Instead spending the night listening to her baby ramble
About the mundane.

Coming home from work,
To put a meal on the table
It was all her
No one else.

So believe me when I say:
Her sweat smells sweet,
Sweeter than honey.

Summer

The sun fills the earth's empty chalice once more
Life returns
The pollen, the hum of the bees
The stings of wasps; of nettles.

As steady as a heart beat
With the harmony of the choir
Summer came without fail
After the death of every spring.

The dried rose petals
Are testaments to our youth
Are something to remember you by;
Without a warm good bye
As sudden as summer
Fall paints the leaves red, orange and plum
Leaving the echoes of our summer.

The Stream

Look at the light
The yellow, amberish hue
One by itself
Will never be enough
But paired with two or three
And the room is bright
What does it mean to be Bright?
To smile so loud, so much that the echoes reverberate
    for days
To have a laugh that is funnier than the joke
To be smart, focused
To be Bright
Is to be a light
And when paired with another
Glows so luminously.

New Me

It's like a mantra
We repeat
New year, New me
A sense of false comfort.

Like we can change in the passing of a minute
Like we can go from poor to rich in a second
That passing of that minute, that second
Isn't end all be all.

I promise,
Change is grating, painful and slow
Change is something that courses in your blood
Burning slow and steady
Until every inch of you has conceded.

So let this new me be full of passion and life
Let it burn in my veins
Deep within my soul
Change will sizzle and sparkle
And in that moment; in that second
I'll see a new me.

To All the Lonely Girls

I don't know when prince charming is coming
Or if he will
Or if he's even real
Lonely lonely girls love books, and movies
Where the girl Always gets the guy
And happy endings for all.

Lonely lonely girls don't give up on love
Even though I have
Lonely lonely girl fall in love with yourself
Lonely lonely girls you are beautiful
You are divine.

Lonely lonely girls maybe you'll get the guy
Maybe you won't
But that's not what defines you
Lonely girls-
Be your own Prince charming
And fall in love.

Blades

I gave you all of my blades,
Handed them to you
Lining them up, glistening under the moonlight
I told you where they'd hurt the most

I stood there
Frail and unarmed
Waiting for you to do the same
To lay down all your blades
To accept our fragility together

How foolish, how human to believe.
Frail and unarmed,
You traced and recounted all the places they'd hurt the most
And dug them deep into me

Under the moonlight
Blood poured and wept
As all the blades were placed into my flesh
That's how you chose to end our friendship.

Wrong

Was it the way I look, the way I smile?
Was it the way my voice echo's in an empty room?
Was it me, all along?
That you hated, despised.

I was so sure, for so long
That I was loved, that I was cherished
And when you said, "I'll be there for you," I thought you meant it
When you said "I love you too."

But I was blinded by adoration
Too blind to see the critical remarks
Digging into my scabbed wounds
Blinded by love
To see that you were laughing at me.

Was it you or I that changed?
And become the other's mortal fear
And now that it has set into motion
All I can do, is sit and wonder: Where it all went wrong.

All The Words I Said To Myself

It's odd
All the things I wanted to hear from others
Never really felt real
Even as my friends and loved ones drowned me in love.

It never felt real
Their words felt empty
There was that distance
Their words couldn't reach me.

It felt so far
So out of grasp; out of reach
So I said it to myself
Maybe then I'll feel it.

So I told myself;
I love you
I built a relationship with the person inside
And I told them all things I wanted to hear.

Words entailing their beauty, their mind and their passion
This act of compassion
All the words;
I said to myself
Made the world less blurry, less dull, less grim

Love isn't instantaneous especially to yourself
It's building yourself up, one word at a time
Until that distance fades away
Day by day.